Friend
or Foe?

Plays About Bullying

By Catherine Gourley

CRABTREE
Publishing Company
www.crabtreebooks.com

Crabtree Publishing Company

www.crabtreebooks.com

Project coordinator: Kathy Middleton
Editor: Reagan Miller
Proofreader: Molly Aloian
Production coordinator: Ken Wright
Prepress technician: Amy Salter
Written, developed, and produced by
RJF Publishing & A+ Media

Project management: Julio Abreu,
    Robert Famighetti
Managing editor: Mark Sachner
Associate editor: Anton Galang
Design: Westgraphix LLC/Tammy West
Illustrations: Spectrum Creative, Inc.

Library and Archives Canada Cataloguing in Publication

Gourley, Catherine, 1950-
    Friend or foe? : plays about bullying / Catherine
Gourlay.

(Get into character)
ISBN 978-0-7787-7363-4 (bound).--ISBN 978-0-7787-7377-1 (pbk.)

    1. Bullying--Juvenile drama. 2. Children's plays,
American. I. Title. II. Series: Get into character

PS3557.O86F75 2010   j812'.54   C2009-906779-X

Library of Congress Cataloging-in-Publication Data

Gourley, Catherine, 1950-
 Friend or foe? : plays about bullying / by Catherine
Gourley.
      p. cm. -- (Get into character)
   ISBN 978-0-7787-7377-1 (pbk. : alk. paper) -- ISBN
978-0-7787-7363-4 (reinforced library binding : alk. paper)
   1. Bullying--Juvenile drama. 2. Children's plays,
American. I. Title. II. Series.

PS3557.O915F75 2009
812'.6--dc22

2009047082

Crabtree Publishing Company

Printed in the USA/122009/BG20091103

www.crabtreebooks.com   1-800-387-7650

**Published in
Canada
Crabtree Publishing**
616 Welland Ave.
St. Catharines, ON
L2M 5V6

**Published in the
United States
Crabtree Publishing**
PMB 59051
350 Fifth Avenue, 59th Floor
New York, New York 10118

**Published in the
United Kingdom
Crabtree Publishing**
Maritime House
Basin Road North, Hove
BN41 1WR

**Published in
Australia
Crabtree Publishing**
386 Mt. Alexander Rd.
Ascot Vale (Melbourne)
VIC 3032

Series Consultants

Reading Consultant: Susan Nations, M.Ed.; Author/Literacy
Coach/Consultant in Literacy Development, Sarasota, Florida.

Content Consultant: Vinita Bhojwani-Patel, Ph.D.; Certified
School/Educational Psychologist, Northfield, Illinois.

Contents

Note to the reader: Be sure to look at the Glossary on page 32 to find definitions of words that might be unfamiliar.

The Newbie

When María, a seventh grader who is new to cell phones and texting, becomes the victim of cyber bullying, she begins to suspect her best friend of starting the rumors about her. When she learns the truth, María also learns a little about herself.

Characters:

Narrators 1, 2, 3

María Martínez, a seventh grade student

Mrs. Martínez, María's mother

Kaylee, María's best friend

Mr. Horrigan, science teacher

Megan, a student at the Center for Math and Science Charter School

Joey, María's biology lab partner

Sweet Pea, an anonymous sender of text messages

Scene 1

Narrator 1: On the last day of summer vacation, María and Kaylee are lying on their matching beach towels at the public pool. They are discussing the most important thing in their lives—the first day of school tomorrow.

Narrator 2: Both girls are going to new schools—Kaylee will enter the seventh grade at John F. Kennedy Middle School. But María has won a scholarship to the Center for Math and Science, a charter school in town. And she's dreading it.

María: I've decided. I'm going to run away.

Kaylee: Where to?

María: Your house.

Kaylee: Don't you think that's the first place your mother will look for you?

María: I'm serious, Kaylee. I never wanted that scholarship. It was my mother's idea.

Kaylee: JFK will be a new school for me, too.

Narrator 3: Kaylee's phone beeps. Quickly, she picks it up, reads the message, and sends a reply.

María: Stop texting. I'm in the middle of a crisis here!

Kaylee: Did you ask your mother again about getting your own cell phone?

María: Every day. It's always the same answer. I don't need a cell phone to talk to my friends.

Narrator 1: That night, however, María's mother surprises her with a back-to-school gift: a new backpack.

Mrs. Martínez: Look inside. I know how nervous you are about tomorrow, and I thought this might cheer you up.

María: My own cell phone? YES! I'm going to text Kaylee!

Mrs. Martínez: Wait one minute. You can only use the phone in school for an emergency. No gossiping. And if I think it's distracting you from your schoolwork—

María: Okay, okay! I get the message!

5

Scene 2

Narrator 2: On the first day of school, Kaylee and María walk in different directions.

Narrator 3: A nervous Kaylee enters the doors of JFK Middle School. Within minutes she sees familiar faces—Tina and Rick. She thinks, "This isn't going to be so bad after all!"

Narrator 1: Across town, however, María is lost. Literally. The charter school is a maze of hallways.

Joey: You a newbie?

María: A what?

Joey: You know, new to Sci High?

María: Oh! Yeah, I'm trying to find Mr. Horrigan's class.

Joey: Biology. I'm going there, too. I'll walk with you.

Scene 3

Mr. Horrigan: Welcome to seventh grade biology, the study of life.

Narrator 2: Mr. Horrigan writes the words "observation" and "question" on the chalkboard.

Mr. Horrigan: In life, an observation provokes a question. And a question leads to . . .?

María: *(calling out)* An answer?

Mr. Horrigan: No . . . a hypothesis.

Narrator 3: The teacher looks at his seating chart.

Mr. Horrigan: Miss María Anna Martínez, correct? You're new here. At this school, students raise their hands when they wish to participate in class.

Narrator 1: María sinks a little in her seat. At that moment, her phone vibrates. She pretends to get something out of her backpack and grabs her phone.

Mr. Horrigan: Miss Martínez.

Narrator 2:	Mr. Horrigan is standing directly behind her. He holds out his hand, palm up.
Mr. Horrigan:	Hand that over, please.
Narrator 3:	She hands over the phone while the other kids snicker.
Narrator 1:	After class, a tall girl approaches María.
Megan:	Don't feel bad. It happens to all of us.
María:	*(gratefully)* Thanks. My first day and I get busted.
Megan:	Oh, and newsflash! Lose the backpack. It's so grade school. Big girls have big bags.
Narrator 2:	Megan spins away, and three other girls follow her. Each carries a large shoulder bag. María wonders if Megan is being nice—or nasty.

Scene 4

Narrator 3:	A week later, Kaylee and María are talking in María's family room after shopping for a shoulder bag. Maria's phone beeps.
María:	That's Joey texting me.
Kaylee:	Joey? Who's he? Is he cute? What's he texting?
Narrator 1:	María pockets her phone.
María:	It's about the biology experiment. He's my lab partner. *(She pauses.)* I failed my first biology quiz!
Kaylee:	But you never fail at anything!
María:	It was on heredity and some hypothesis about mung beans. I haven't told my mother.
Kaylee:	Mung beans?
María:	They're a type of pea. We're growing them in our bio lab.
Kaylee:	Next time, text me with the questions and I'll text you the answers.
María:	*(sarcastically)* Oh right, like you're going to know all about seeds and germination.

Kaylee: Hey, I might. You're not the only one who has a brain. Don't go getting, you know, too good for us now that you're going to that fancy school.

Narrator 2: That night, María receives a text message from an unfamiliar phone number. The message says:

Sweet Pea: *(texted message)* Newbie—how did you get into Sci High? Cheat on the entrance exam? XOXO, Sweet Pea.

Narrator 3: María stares at the message, and wonders. . . . If Kaylee is teasing her, it's a pretty mean thing to say.

Scene 5

Narrator 1: Texting begins to dominate María's life. She texts at the breakfast table, during lunch, and after school. She gets hundreds of messages every day.

Narrator 2: The mysterious Sweet Pea texts María over and over. Those messages are getting meaner, making fun of María's behavior and her clothing. María thinks about telling someone, but she doesn't know who to trust.

Mrs. Martínez: How was your day?

Narrator 3: María doesn't answer. She's texting a message to Joey. Her mother reaches for the phone.

María: Mom! That's private!

Mrs. Martínez: I'm not going to read it. I just need your undivided attention. I had a call from Mr. Horrigan today.

María: He doesn't like me. He thinks because I came from public school I'm stupid. Everyone there thinks it.

Mrs. Martínez: Actually, he seemed concerned about you, that maybe you were having trouble adjusting to the new school. Do you want to talk about it?

Narrator 1: María is afraid her mother will take the phone away from her.

Mrs. Martínez: Have you made friends?

María: Just Joey. He was a newbie last year. He says it'll get better.

Mrs. Martínez: He's right.

Narrator 2: Only it doesn't get better. That night it gets worse. María receives another message from Sweet Pea:

Sweet Pea: (texting) No one likes you. You should just run away.

Scene 6

Narrator 3: María finally decides that she needs to say something to Kaylee about the messages she's been getting from Sweet Pea:

María: (texting to Kaylee) Do you have another cell phone you're texting from? Are you the one?

Kaylee: (texting back) The one what?

María: Sending those horrible messages about me?

Kaylee: You're my BFF. Why would I say bad things about you?

María: Because you're jealous.

Narrator 1: María waits for Kaylee's response. But Kaylee has stopped texting.

Scene 7

Narrator 2: At the end of the month, Mrs. Martínez receives her phone bill. She is stunned to see that María has sent more than 2,000 text messages. She confronts her.

Mrs. Martínez: María, I can't afford this! I'll have to take your cell away if you can't use it more responsibly. Besides, I think it's interfering with your school work.

María: Why do I always have to do things your way? I'm going to flunk out, and there isn't anything you can do about it. And I don't care. I hate that school! And they hate me!

Narrator 3: María runs out of the room. The angry outburst both surprises and confuses her mother.

Mrs. Martínez: (says to herself) Is she trying to fail?

Narrator 1: On the kitchen table, the cell phone begins to beep. She doesn't want to pry into her daughter's life, but clearly María is upset by something. Mrs. Martínez presses Read. She sees a message:

Sweet Pea: *(texted message)* Go back to where you came from.

Narrator 2: Her mother knocks softly on María's door.

Mrs. Martínez: María? Who's Sweet Pea?

Scene 8

Narrator 3: For the first time in weeks, María and her mother talk. María tells her about the text messages and that she thinks Kaylee is sending them. Kaylee knows about the mung bean experiment. She knows about failed biology quizzes and about Joey.

María: *(pleading)* Please don't make me go back to that school!

Mrs. Martínez: I won't make you go back if you feel so strongly about it. But María, running away won't make the problem go away. This isn't about you being inferior, because you're not. It's about Sweet Pea trying to make you feel inferior. Looks like she—or he—is succeeding.

María: So what do I do?

Mrs. Martínez: Do you remember what Mr. Horrigan said about the importance of careful observation to test a theory? *(María nods.)* Did you save Sweet Pea's messages?

María: Some of them.

Mrs. Martínez: Do you want to share them with me? We can reread them and look for clues.

Narrator 1: María calms down. Once she rereads the messages with her brain and not her emotions, it doesn't take very long to solve the mystery.

Sweet Pea: *(texted message)* Newsflash to Anna—that skirt is way too short. Not even Joey is interested in your spaghetti legs.

María: It couldn't have been Kaylee. She didn't know what I was wearing that day. And she'd never, never call me by my middle name, Anna! It's got to be Megan!

Narrator 2: Mrs. Martínez remembers. Megan was why María had insisted on having a big bag instead of her backpack.

María: So now what do I do?

Mrs. Martínez: You have a choice. You can confront her or ignore her.

María: Ignore her? It's that simple?

Mrs. Martínez: Not really, but once you recognize that bullying is about controlling another person, it's a lot easier to cope with it. Megan can't hurt you if you turn off what she says. But you have to turn it off up here, too.

Narrator 3: Mrs. Martínez touches María's forehead. Then she hands her the phone.

Mrs. Martínez: I think you have a real friend who needs to hear from you. Call Kaylee.

María: But Mom! What if she's blocked me!

Mrs. Martínez: In that case, I guess you'll just have to walk to her house and talk to her in person. Just like old times.

María: Just like old times! I like that.

Narrator 1: María grabs her jacket and goes—leaving her cell phone behind.

The End

Think It Over

1. In Scene 3, María wonders if Megan's comments were intended to be nice or nasty. What do you think was Megan's intention?

2. Why does María suspect her best friend Kaylee has been sending the nasty messages to her? What evidence might María have to support this "false" assumption?

3. María's mother says Sweet Pea's messages are not about María's inferiority. They are a way for Sweet Pea to make María feel inferior. Why would someone want to make another person feel inferior?

4. Once María strongly suspects she knows the identity of Sweet Pea, her mother says that one way of handling the problem is not to be confrontational but rather to ignore her. In your opinion, would this be the best way to handle María's problem? Tell why or why not.

5. María's mother says María does not have to stay in the charter school. Do you think she will stay or return to public school? If you were María, what would you want to do?

The Secret Life of a Bully

Kids laugh at J.J.'s jokes, but not because they think he's funny. They want to avoid being pushed around by him. J.J.'s confrontation with an outspoken girl and a gutsy smaller kid help J.J. change his behavior.

Characters:

Narrators 1, 2, 3

Mike Palance

Jared "J.J." Jones

Karen Costello

Lou Jones, *J.J.'s father*

Justin

Tyler

Mrs. Ashland,
middle school guidance counselor

Principal

Scene 1

Narrator 1: In the cafeteria of Parkrose Middle School, Mike Palance slides his tray toward the cash register.

Narrator 2: He looks over his shoulder, a little fearfully. "So far, so good," he thinks. Maybe this morning he'll actually get through the line before—

J.J.: *(loudly)* Make way! Coming through!

Narrator 3: Mike carries his tray to the cash register and hurriedly pays for his lunch.

Narrator 1: J.J. cuts the line in front of Karen Costello and directly behind Mike.

Karen: Excuse me, what are you doing? Go to the back of the line!

J.J.: I got to talk to my best bud here.

Narrator 2: J.J. puts a meaty hand on Mike's shoulder.

J.J.: Give me your money, kid. I'm extra hungry today.

Mike: *(triumphantly)* Too late, J.J. I already spent it.

Narrator 3: Mike walks across the noisy cafeteria to a table. J.J. follows him. He sits down opposite Mike.

Narrator 1: Two other boys who were eating at the table leave.

J.J.: That's real considerate of you, Mike. Buying me lunch.

Narrator 2: J.J. slides the lunch tray away from Mike. He picks up the burger and takes a big bite.

Narrator 3: Mike watches as J.J. eats his lunch—again!

J.J.: You can have the apple. I don't like apples.

Mike: No thanks. I lost my appetite.

Narrator 1: While leaving the cafeteria for the next class, Karen walks beside Mike.

Karen: Why do you let him walk all over you like that?

Mike: Are you blind, Karen? He's bigger than me, and I'd rather not get my butt kicked.

Karen: *(shaking her head and muttering)* He's such bully!

Scene 2

Narrator 2: That night, J.J. is at home taking out the garbage. The bag splits. Wet garbage spills over the kitchen floor.

Lou Jones: Now look at what you did! What's the matter with you?

J.J.: I didn't do it on purpose.

Lou Jones: How many times have I told you not to overload the bag? You never listen!

Narrator 3: As J.J. cleans up the mess, he mutters to himself: "It's only garbage."

Lou Jones: What did you say?

J.J.: I said it's only garbage.

Lou Jones: You giving me lip?

Narrator 1: J.J. sees that "look" in his father's face, the one that tells J.J. if he says one more word, he's crossed the line.

J.J.: Sorry.

Lou Jones: You're sorry, all right. Sometimes I wonder, J.J. I wonder what you're good for.

Narrator 2: Apparently not for taking out the garbage, J.J. thinks. But he says nothing more.

Scene 3

Narrator 3: The next day, at the back of the room in English class, Karen overhears J.J. telling a joke.

J.J.: Okay. I've got a knock-knock joke. Everyone listening?

Narrator 1: Justin and Tyler are leaning forward with anticipation.

J.J.: Knock knock.

Justin: Who's there?

J.J.: Mikey.

Tyler: Mikey who?

J.J.: Mikey Mouse!

Narrator 2: Justin and Tyler grin foolishly, but they aren't sure they get it.

J.J.: Get it? Mikey? As in *Mike*?

Narrator 3: Now Justin and Tyler laugh hysterically.
The teacher turns and glares.

Karen: *(shaking her head)* Lame.

Scene 4

Narrator 1: Later that day during lunch, Mike hands J.J. two dollars before J.J. even says a word. Mike pulls a sandwich out of a bag and sits down to eat.

Narrator 2: But J.J. isn't satisfied. He takes one half of Mike's sandwich and starts to devour it. The kids at the other tables laugh.

Narrator 3: Mike gets up to move away, but J.J. puts his hand on his shoulder and forces him back into his seat— harder than J.J. intended. The action surprises them both.

Narrator 1: The laughter stops. J.J. sees that the others are watching him, waiting.

Justin: Go on, J.J. Show the runt who's in charge.

Narrator 2: J.J. hesitates. He doesn't want to fight Mike. He just wants to have some fun.

Narrator 3: J.J. takes the rest of Mike's sandwich and shoves that into his mouth, too.

Karen: Nobody thinks you're funny, J.J.

J.J.: No? Then why are they laughing?

Narrator 1: J.J. walks to where Tyler is sitting. He pokes him in the shoulder.

J.J.: Hey, Tyler, you think I'm funny, don't you?

. . . J.J. ISN'T SATISFIED. HE TAKES ONE HALF OF MIKE'S SANDWICH AND STARTS TO DEVOUR IT. THE KIDS AT THE OTHER TABLES LAUGH.

Narrator 2: Tyler looks around, a little wild-eyed. J.J. pokes him again, a little harder.

Tyler: Sure, J.J. You're funny.

J.J.: *(to Karen)* See?

Karen: The only reason Tyler laughs at you is because he's afraid of you.

Tyler: No I'm not!

Narrator 3: J.J. barks like a mean dog at Karen. Once again, the other boys laugh.

Scene 5

Narrator 1: Later in the day, Karen knocks on the door to the guidance counselor's office. She tells Mrs. Ashland she knows someone who is being bullied.

Narrator 2: Mrs. Ashland listens as Karen describes the daily confrontations between J.J. and Mike.

Mrs. Ashland: Why do you think he picks on Mike?

Karen: Mike's smart. He's smaller. And he doesn't fight back.

Narrator 3: A commotion in the hallway startles them. Mrs. Ashland opens her office door. A student with a bloody nose is holding a paper towel to his face, and a teacher is hurrying him to the nurse. The boy with the bloody nose is Tyler.

Narrator 1: Following the nurse and Tyler comes the principal, who is walking ahead of J.J. As he walks by, J.J. sees Karen standing in the guidance counselor's office, watching him.

Narrator 2: Inside the principal's office, J.J. slouches in a chair.

J.J.: I didn't want to fight.

Principal: Then why did you?

J.J.: Someone said Tyler was afraid of me. So after gym class, Tyler challenged me. What else could I do? I had to fight back.

Principal: You could have walked away.

AS HE WALKS BY, J.J. SEES KAREN STANDING IN THE GUIDANCE COUNSELOR'S OFFICE, WATCHING HIM.

J.J.: Babies walk away.

Principal: You've got it backward, J.J. A smart person walks away rather than get pushed into doing something he knows is wrong. He doesn't take advantage of someone he knows he can hurt.

J.J.: You're going to call my father, aren't you?

Principal: Fighting in school is an automatic suspension. You know that, J.J.

Scene 6

Narrator 3: Three days later, J.J. is once again in the principal's office. With him is his father.

Lou Jones: It was just boys' play. They're starting to grow up. And at this age, they're bound to get into fights.

Principal: Not all boys fight, Mr. Jones. And not all fights are just boys' play.

Lou Jones: My son didn't start this. That boy came after him. J.J. only did what I taught him to do—stand up for himself. I don't need you to tell me how to raise my son.

Mrs. Ashland: We have students who tell us that J.J. bullies other children on a daily basis.

J.J.: (surprised) Who told you that?

Mrs. Ashland: He takes money from them. He steals their food. He waits for them by their lockers to intimidate them.

Lou Jones: Is that right, J.J.? You steal things?

Narrator 1: J.J. looks at the wall. He doesn't answer.

Lou Jones: (angrily) You look at me when I speak!

Narrator 2: Mrs. Ashland is beginning to understand where J.J. has learned his bullying behavior.

Mrs. Ashland: Bullying isn't about being strong or weak, Mr. Jones. It's about controlling another person.

Lou Jones: *(to J.J.)* No son of mine is going to be a punk thief. *(to the principal and counselor)* You have my word, this won't happen again. J.J. won't give you any more trouble. Is that all? I have to get back to work. You understand, don't you?

Principal: Yes. I think we do understand now.

Lou Jones: *(to J.J.)* You and I—we'll settle this at home.

Narrator 3: J.J.'s father has gone, but the principal still has not dismissed him.

Principal: Your father is right about one thing. You are growing up, finding out who you are. But you don't grow up by stepping on other people, J.J.

Scene 7

Narrator 1: After school, J.J. waits for Karen at her locker.

J.J.: What did you tell Mrs. Ashland about me?

Karen: I didn't get you in trouble, J.J. You did that all by yourself.

J.J.: Why did you go to her? I didn't do anything to you!

Karen: Because I don't like the way you treat Mike. You have no feelings, J.J. You don't know what it's like to be put down every day.

J.J: Oh, don't I? That's where you're wrong. Because I do know!

Karen: *(surprised)* Then . . . why do you do it?

Narrator 2: Mike turns the corner. He sees J.J. glaring at Karen. Suddenly, Mike doesn't care if he gets his butt kicked. He's not going to let J.J. bully him—or anyone—anymore.

Mike: Leave her alone, J.J.

Karen: It's OK, Mike. We're just talking.

Mike: No, it's not OK. *(to J.J.)* You want money? You'll have to fight me for it.

J.J.: I don't want your money.

Narrator 3: Mike pushes J.J. Any other time, J.J. would have pushed back. But not today.

Narrator 1: A crowd has gathered. J.J. looks at them. Some of the kids are amused. A whole lot more are not. "They don't like me," J.J. realizes. "Karen's right. They are laughing at me."

Karen: Mike, you don't have to do this.

Mike: Yes, I do!

J.J.: No, you don't.

Narrator 2: J.J. knows what it feels like to be bullied day after day. And he doesn't like it one bit. J.J. makes a decision.

Narrator 3: The crowd is waiting. But this time, J.J. disappoints some and surprises others. He turns and walks away.

The End

Think It Over

1. Describe the relationship J.J. has with his father.

2. In your opinion, why does J.J. intimidate Mike? And why does Mike give in so easily?

3. Mrs. Ashland says that bullying isn't about being strong. It's about controlling another person. Who controls J.J.? How does this person control J.J.?

4. When Karen asks J.J. why he bullies people when he himself knows how it feels, he doesn't answer. What do you think is the answer to Karen's question?

5. In the final scene, Karen tells Mike that he doesn't have to fight J.J. But Mike says he does. In your opinion, what options did Mike have? How else might he have gotten J.J. to stop his bullying?

Your Turn

1. Which of these two stories is closest to one of your or your friends' experiences at school? Write a short paper explaining how you could change one (or both) of the stories with a different, more positive ending.

2. Both stories have characters who are parents. Write a compare-and-contrast paper on María's mother and J.J.'s father. What are their character traits? What flaws do they have? Which parent, if any, understands what their child is feeling?

3. Select one scene from one of the plays and rewrite it, using dialogue, from the viewpoint of another character.

Glossary

commotion A great deal of noise, an uproar

devour To eat hungrily, quickly, and eagerly

germination Growing from a seed into an individual plant or being

heredity The transfer of characteristics, such as eye color, passed from one generation to the next

hypothesis A theory, an assumption

intimidate To bully, threaten

snicker Giggle, laugh in a mocking way

triumphantly Victoriously, successfully

wild-eyed With a look of panic or desperation

About the Author

Catherine Gourley is the author of the award-winning nonfiction series *Women's Images and Issues of the 20th Century: How Popular Culture Portrayed Women in the 20th Century*. She is the national director of Letters About Literature, a reading promotion program of the Center for the Book in the Library of Congress.